SIMPLY CLASSICS

GRADES 0–1

Arrangements for piano solo
by **Peter Gritton**

Series editor Anthony Williams

FABER *ff* MUSIC

PREFACE

I can't wait for you to get your fingers around the *Simply Classics* series! It has been an exciting task selecting the music. Arrangements get harder as you progress through the volume, giving a sense of gradual achievement and helping you to select pieces of an appropriate standard.

The main reason for *Simply Classics'* existence is to encourage exposure to great music. Anyone who has tried arranging classics for beginners will be aware that although simplified they must remain musically complete. Staying true to each composer's intention is very important, and in shortening pieces, great effort has been made to give each a sense of completeness and shape.

The ability to play in a range of styles will help to develop a variety of touch and timbre as well as to develop knowledge and understanding of three hundred years' worth of music! The earliest piece in the volume – Monteverdi's *Fanfare from L'Orfeo* (1607) – needs brilliance and clarity in the outer sections and controlled beauty of tone in the middle. The latest piece, Dvořák's *New World Symphony* (1893), requires a warmth in the sound borne out of listening and a relaxed but firm touch. The Baroque era is represented by five pieces, including Arne's world-renowned *Rule, Britannia!* – independence of hands is of the essence here. Mozart's *Eine kleine Nachtmusik*, Haydn's *The Surprise Symphony* and Beethoven's *Violin Concerto* most adequately represent the Classical era – all requiring a clarity of touch. The twelve Romantic pieces typify the quite extraordinary spectrum of styles – from Schubert's sublime *Rosamunde* to Bizet's *Toreador Song*, Wagner's *Siegfried's Horn Call* and Mussorgsky's *Promenade* – to name but a few!

Peter Gritton

© 2007 by Faber Music Ltd
This edition first published in 2007
3 Queen Square London WC1N 3AU
Music processed by Jeanne Roberts
Cover design by Kenosha
Printed in England by Caligraving Ltd
All rights reserved

ISBN 0-571-52551-2

To buy Faber Music publications or to find out about the full range of titles available
please contact your local music retailer or Faber Music sales enquiries:

Faber Music Ltd, Burnt Mill, Elizabeth Way, Harlow CM20 2HX
Tel: +44 (0) 1279 82 89 82   Fax: +44 (0) 1279 82 89 83
sales@fabermusic.com   fabermusic.com

CONTENTS

PASSACAGLIA   JS BACH   *page 4*

RULE, BRITANNIA!   ARNE   *page 5*

VIOLIN CONCERTO   BEETHOVEN   *page 6*

SYMPHONY NO.1   BRAHMS   *page 7*

PROMENADE   MUSSORGSKY   *page 8*

SIEGFRIED'S HORN CALL   WAGNER   *page 9*

TOREADOR SONG   BIZET   *page 10*

LULLABY   BRAHMS   *page 11*

POLOVTSIAN DANCE   BORODIN   *page 12*

THE TROUT   SCHUBERT   *page 13*

CAVATINA   DVOŘÁK   *page 14*

NEW WORLD SYMPHONY   DVOŘÁK   *page 15*

OVERTURE TO MUSIC FOR THE ROYAL FIREWORKS   HANDEL   *page 16*

MUSIC FOR THE ROYAL FIREWORKS MINUET NO.2   HANDEL   *page 17*

THE SURPRISE SYMPHONY   HAYDN   *page 18*

ROSAMUNDE   SCHUBERT   *page 19*

FANFARE FROM *L'ORFEO*   MONTEVERDI   *page 20*

LA DONNA È MOBILE   VERDI   *page 22*

EINE KLEINE NACHTMUSIK   MOZART   *page 23*

OVERTURE TO *WILLIAM TELL*   ROSSINI   *page 24*

Passacaglia
Theme

Composer's nationality **German**   *Era* **Baroque**
Date of piece **c.1705**   *Originally for* **organ**

'Passacaglia' is an Italian word for 'walking down the street'. This one has a bit of a limp! Can you spot where the melody moves from right to left hand in the last line?

Johann Sebastian Bach
1685–1750

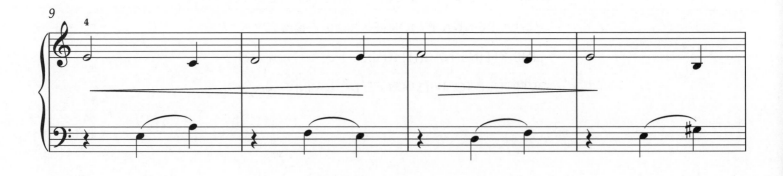

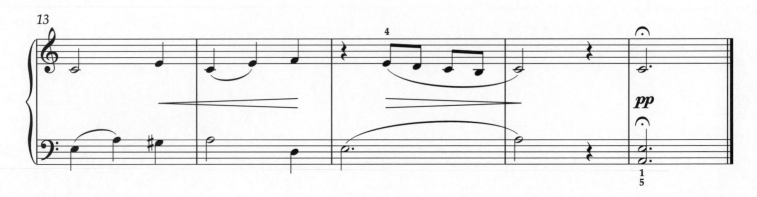

Rule, Britannia!

from *Alfred*

Composer's nationality **British**   *Era* **Baroque**
Date of piece **1740**   *Originally from a* **play with music**

Thomas Arne wrote this famous song over two hundred and fifty years ago
and it is still one of the highlights of *The Last Night of the Proms*.

Thomas Arne
1710–1778

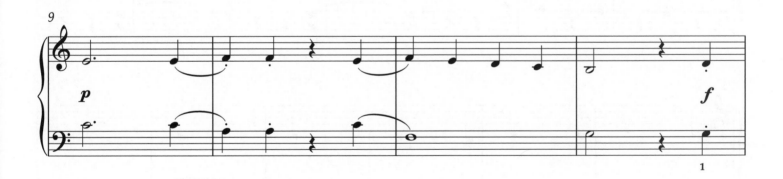

Violin Concerto

Rondo theme (third movement)

Composer's nationality **German** Era **Classical**
Date of piece **1806** Originally for **violin and orchestra**

This is the beginning of the rousing rondo that Beethoven ends his *Violin Concerto*
with. He loved using this merry dance style because it sounded fun.

Ludwig van Beethoven
1770–1827

Symphony No. 1

from the finale

Brahms wrote four huge symphonies for full orchestra. This theme from the finale to Symphony No.1 sounds like the ringing of bells.

Composer's nationality **German** Era **Romantic**
Date of piece **1855–76** Originally for **orchestra**

Johannes Brahms
1833–1897

Promenade

from *Pictures at an Exhibition*

Composer's nationality **Russian**   Era **Romantic**
Date of piece **1874**   Originally a **piano solo**

This was originally a piano piece, but most people know it as an arrangement for orchestra by Ravel. It is a musical description of someone walking around an art gallery.

Modest Mussorgsky
1839–1881

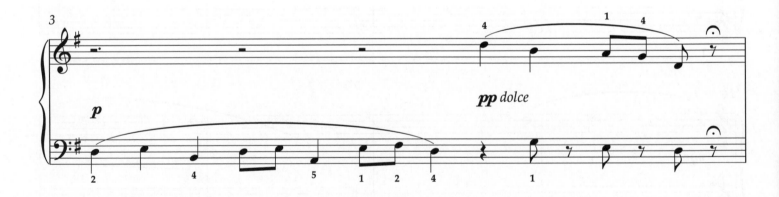

Siegfried's Horn Call

from *Siegfried*

Composer's nationality **German** Era **Romantic**
Date of piece **1856–57** Originally from an **opera**

Wagner wrote operas that were so difficult to stage that he decided to build his own
theatre! In a couple of these operas, we hear of the adventures of the hero Siegfried.
This french horn fanfare shows just how heroic he was.

Richard Wagner
1813–1883

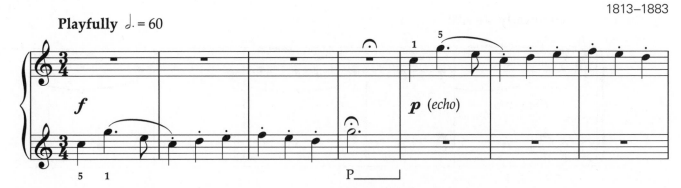

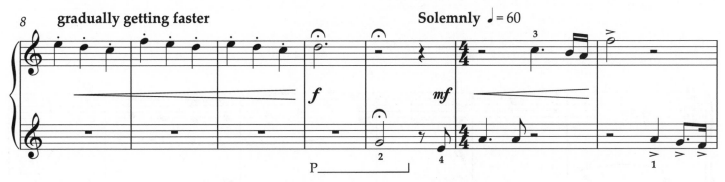

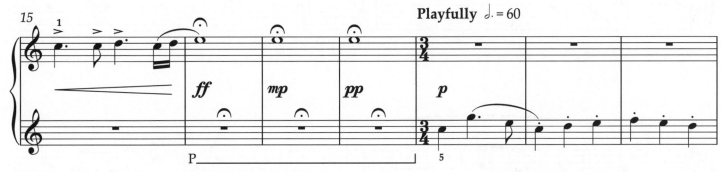

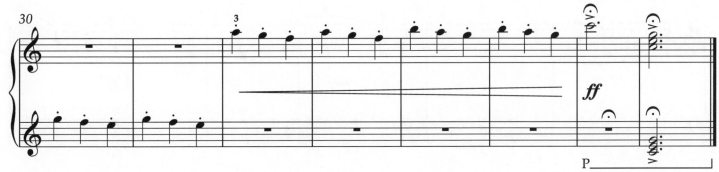

Toreador Song

from *Carmen*

Composer's nationality **French** *Era* **Romantic**
Date of piece **1873–74** *Originally an* **opera aria**

This is a tune from one of the most famous operas, *Carmen*. The composer, Bizet,
died in the same year as the first performance so never knew how popular it was
going to be.

Georges Bizet
1838–1875

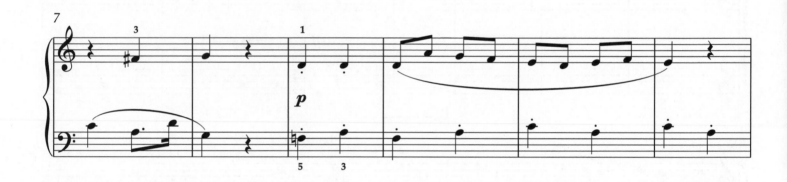

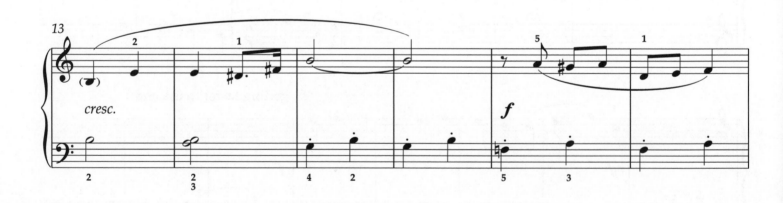

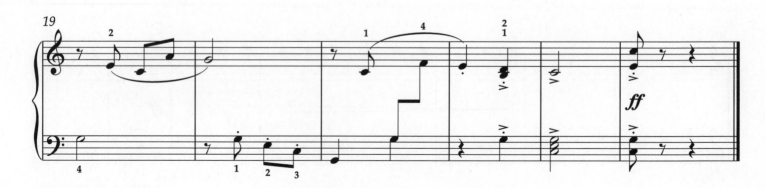

Lullaby

Composer's nationality **German** *Era* **Romantic**
Date of piece **1868** *Originally for* **voice and piano**

Some people think that this simple lullaby is a folk song. Actually, it was written by
one of the most famous composers ever – Johannes Brahms.

Johannes Brahms
1833–1897

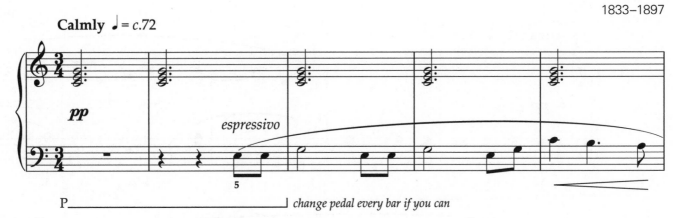

Polovtsian Dance

from *Prince Igor*

Composer's nationality **Russian**   *Era* **Romantic**
Date of piece **1875**   *Originally from an* **opera**

This well-known Russian dance comes from the opera *Prince Igor*. Borodin never
managed to finish the opera, even though he tried for nearly twenty years!

Alexander Borodin
1833–1887

The Trout

Composer's nationality **Austrian**   Era **Romantic**
Date of piece **1817**   Originally for **voice and piano**

Schubert wrote many songs for voice and piano, of which *The Trout* is perhaps
the most popular. He was also paid to compose a set of variations on the tune
for piano quintet.

Franz Schubert
1797–1828

Cavatina

No. 1 from *Miniatures*

| Composer's nationality **Czech** | Era **Romantic** |
| Date of piece **1887** | Originally for **string trio** |

Cavatina is a little piece that was originally written for two violins and one viola – a bit like a string quartet minus the cello. Perhaps the cellist was having a night off!

Antonín Dvořák
1841–1904

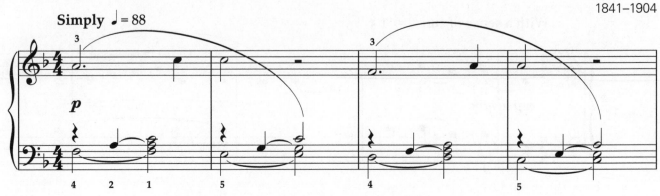

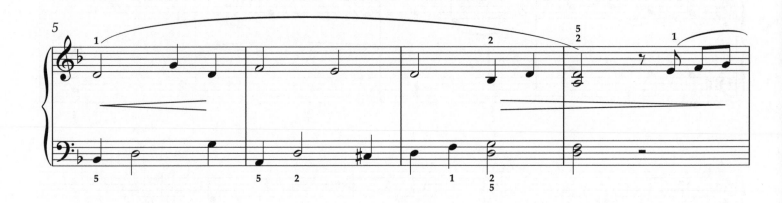

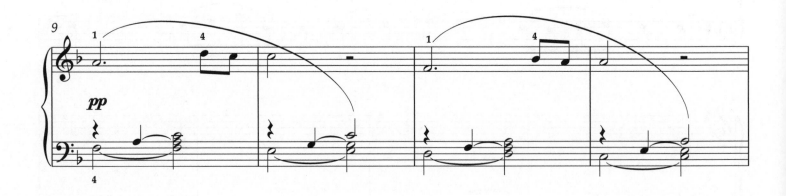

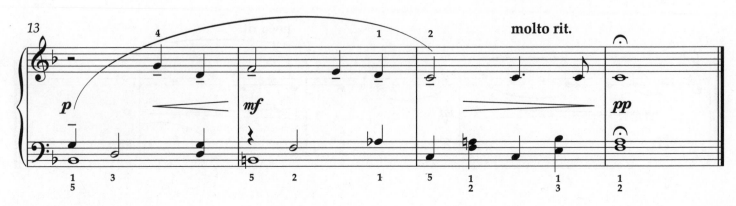

New World Symphony

Second movement theme

Composer's nationality **Czech**   *Era* **Romantic**
Date of piece **1893**   *Originally for* **orchestra**

This tune is from a symphony called *From the New World*. The 'New World' is the old
name for America, which is where the composer was living at the time.

Antonín Dvořák
1841–1904

Overture to
Music for the Royal Fireworks

Composer's nationality **German**	Era **Baroque**
Date of piece **1749**	Originally for **wind band**

In 1749, Handel was asked to write some exciting music to accompany a huge fireworks display. Apparently the fireworks went wrong, but the music still sounded spectacular!

George Frideric Handel
1685–1759

Music for the Royal Fireworks

Minuet No. 2

Composer's nationality **German**   Era **Baroque**
Date of piece **1749**   Originally for **wind band**

Handel's *Music for the Royal Fireworks* was so popular that 12,000 people turned up to the final rehearsal, bringing 18th century London to a standstill!

George Frideric Handel
1685–1759

The Surprise Symphony

Slow movement theme

Composer's nationality **Austrian** Era **Classical**
Date of piece **1791** Originally for **orchestra**

Haydn wrote 104 symphonies, many of which have interesting nicknames. This is the theme to a set of variations from a symphony called *The Surprise* – can you see why?

Franz Joseph Haydn
1732–1809

Rosamunde

Composer's nationality **Austrian**	*Era* **Romantic**
Date of piece **1823**	*Originally for* **orchestra**

We are very lucky that this beautiful tune survives because the manuscript
was lost for many years. It was written as a musical interlude for a play.

Franz Schubert
1797–1828

Fanfare from *L'Orfeo*

Composer's nationality **Italian** *Era* **Renaissance/Baroque**
Date of piece **1607** *Originally from an* **opera**

Monteverdi wrote this fanfare to start *L'Orfeo* – an opera about Orpheus in the
underworld. The loud bars are played by brass; the quiet bars in the middle by strings.

Claudio Monteverdi
1567–1643

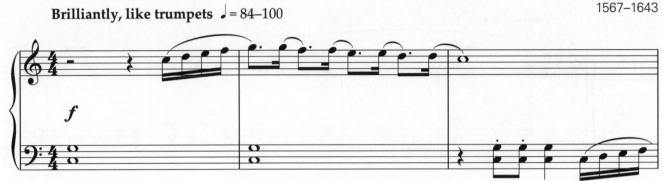

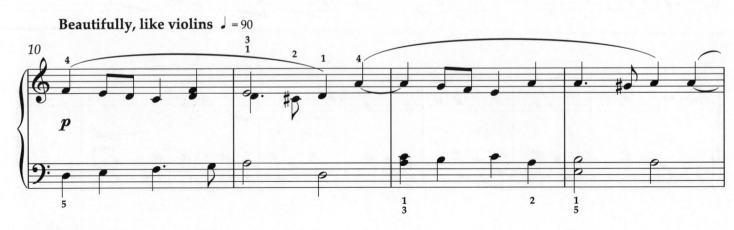

Brilliantly, as before ♩ = 84–100

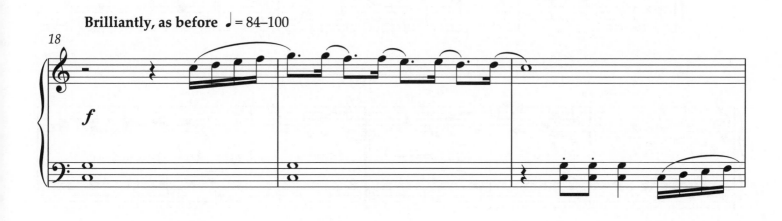

molto rit.

La donna è mobile

from *Rigoletto*

Composer's nationality **Italian**   *Era* **Romantic**
Date of piece **1850–51**   *Originally an* **opera aria**

In 19th century Italy, Verdi's tunes were the pop music of the day.
This bouncy tune is usually sung by a dramatic tenor voice!

Giuseppe Verdi
1813–1901

Eine kleine Nachtmusik

First movement

Composer's nationality **Austrian**   *Era* **Classical**
Date of piece **1787**   *Originally for* **string orchestra**

This very famous tune is the opening of a serenade called *A Little Night Music*.
In Mozart's language, German, it is *Eine kleine Nachtmusik*.

Wolfgang Amadeus Mozart
1756–1791

Overture to *William Tell*

Composer's nationality **Italian** *Era* **Romantic**
Date of piece **1829** *Originally from an* **opera**

Rossini's opera *William Tell* is best known for this overture, and especially this theme.
It's amazing how exciting even the quiet bits are – music doesn't need to be loud to
be thrilling!

Gioachino Rossini
1792–1868

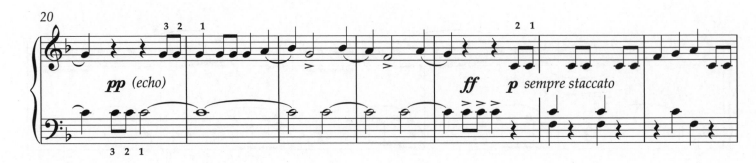